A Little Greek Cookbook

Rena Salaman

First published in 1990 by
The Appletree Press Ltd, 7 James Street South,
Belfast BT2 8DL.
Copyright © 1990 The Appletree Press, Ltd. Illustrations ©
1990 Metin Salih used under Exclusive License to
The Appletree Press, Ltd.
Printed in Hong Kong. All rights reserved.
No part of this publication may be
reproduced or transmitted in any form
or by means, electronic or mechanical,
photocopying, recording or any information
and retrieval system, without permission in
writing from the publisher

First published in the United States in 1990
by Chronicle Books, 275 Fifth Street,
San Francisco, CA 94103

ISBN: 0-87701-795-6

9 8 7 6 5 4 3 2 1

Introduction

When Greeks cook, the emphasis is on people getting together, on conviviality, on sociability, and celebration. Food is consumed in a leisurely way to keep the conversation flowing and spirits rising and to allow the diners to indulge in nostalgia and reminisce about times long past – childhood, wars fought, children baptized or married. When Greeks gather round a table their behavior shows their shared characteristics: an extravagant generosity, a high sense of honor – the famous *philotimo* – an impatience with the formal, a spontaneous enthusiasm for the personal and the emotional. In the years to come, both the meal and the occasion will be remembered and reminisced about. It is around food and the table that Greek life unfolds and revolves. Greek food, in short, is a celebration both of food and people.

A note on measures
Spoon measurements are level except where otherwise indicated. Seasonings can of course be adjusted according to taste. Recipes are for four.

Taramosalata

Taramosalata has travelled far and has become a familiar favorite in many foreign countries. Originally used as a convenient dish when refrigerators did not exist, it is made with *tarama*, the dried and salted roe of large fish such as grey mullet, which comes from Messolonghi in western Greece. An excellent alternative is fresh smoked cod's roe which keeps in the refrigerator 4-5 days. In Greece, Taramosalata is mostly eaten in the winter and particularly during Lent, when most people are fasting. Serve it as Greeks do as a tempting starter with a simple main course such as bean or lentil soup.

---

4 thick slices stale white bread, crusts removed
6 oz fresh smoked cod's roe
½ cup olive oil
1 ½ lemons
1 thin slice of onion
a few black olives to garnish

Soak the bread in water for 15 minutes. Squeeze it a little to extract some of the moisture and put it in a food processor or blender. Skin the fresh roe and add it to the bread with the lemon juice and the onion. Blend well, adding the oil slowly while the blades are running. Taste and adjust seasoning. If a milder taste is preferred, add a little more bread and oil. If too stiff add a little water as it should be of a rather creamy consistency. Spread on a platter with the olives piled in the center.

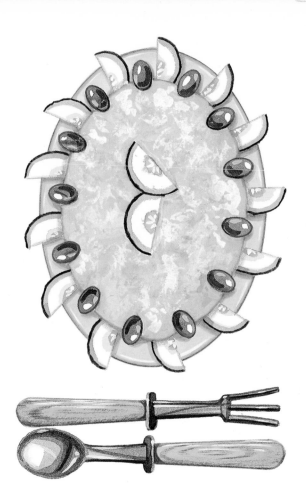

Keftethes

Fried Minced Meat Balls

When Keftethes are being fried the most appetizing aromas are released from the kitchen over the whole neighborhood. They are served as part of *mezethes* (starters) or with a simple main course to add variety to the table. They are absolutely delicious when made with minced lamb.

---

1 lb minced lamb or beef
2 medium slices crustless stale white bread, soaked briefly in water
1 medium onion, thickly grated
1 tbsp fresh chopped mint or ½ tsp dried mint
2 tbsp chopped parsley
1 egg
salt and freshly ground pepper
¾ cup plain flour
5 tbsp sunflower oil for frying

Squeeze out excess water from bread and combine with remaining ingredients in a bowl. Mix well and make walnut-shaped balls. At this stage they can rest. Just before they are to be served roll them lightly in flour and fry in hot oil for 3-4 minutes until golden all over. They can be shallow or deep-fried.

Tzatziki

Yogurt and Cucumber Salad

Fried slices of aubergines and courgettes and a plate of olives are often offered with refreshing Tzatziki. It can also accompany roasts and grills. Try using a thick, preferably sheep's, yogurt to give a unique flavor and texture to the dish.

---

2 tbsp olive oil
1 tsp white wine vinegar
1 clove garlic, peeled and crushed
1 cup plain, thick yogurt
5 in cucumber, peeled and finely diced or coarsely grated
1½ tbsp finely chopped fresh mint or ½ tsp dried mint, crumbled
salt

Beat oil, vinegar, and garlic lightly in a bowl, using a fork. Add yogurt and salt and beat lightly, until well amalgamated and smooth. Mix in the cucumber and the mint and lightly chill before serving.

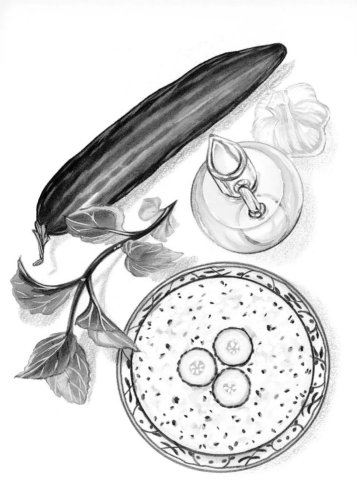

Melitzanosalata

Aubergine Salad

Summer in Greece cannot be conceived of without the exotic aubergine which has become a symbol of all Mediterranean summer cooking. Melitzanosalata appears with *mezethes* in most restaurants. Serve it with toasted bread or crisp pita bread. Covered, it keeps for 3-4 days in the refrigerator.

1½ lb aubergines (2 large ones)
2 cloves garlic, peeled and sliced
5 tbsp olive oil
juice of 1 lemon
salt and freshly ground pepper
2 tbsp plain yogurt
parsley sprigs and black olives to garnish

Rinse and dry the aubergines. Prick them with a fork, otherwise they may explode in the oven, and cook them at 350°F for one hour, turning them occasionally. When the aubergines are cool, cut in half, scrape out the flesh into a sieve, and press lightly to extract the bitter juices. Then place the flesh in a blender with the rest of the ingredients, except for oil and yogurt, and blend, adding the oil slowly, until quite smooth. Mix in the yogurt, taste and adjust seasoning. Serve on a pretty platter, decorated with olives and a sprig or two of parsley.

Kolokythakia kai Melitzanes Skorthalia

Fried Courgettes and Aubergines with Garlic Sauce

This is an essentially Greek island dish, served with home-baked bread as a main course. Families help themselves from a central platter as they consume the savory slices one after the other. It is best served with the vegetables freshly fried and hot, but it could wait for up to one hour if needed.

---

12 oz aubergines, trimmed, washed and sliced in rounds
12 oz courgettes, scraped lightly, washed, and sliced lengthwise
2 tbsp plain flour to coat the vegetables
sunflower oil for frying
salt

Slice courgettes into approximately ¼ in thick, long slices. Immerse aubergines in lightly salted water for 30 minutes. Rinse, squeeze gently, and pat dry. Dust courgette slices lightly with flour and fry in the hot oil until pale golden on both sides. Drain on absorbent paper. Aubergines need quite hot oil, otherwise they absorb it instantly so refill frying pan with oil, raise heat, dust slices in flour and fry in batches until golden brown. Drain on absorbent kitchen paper. Arrange vegetables on a platter, season with salt and, just before serving, decorate with Skorthalia (see page 15).

Skorthalia

Garlic Dip

This is a frugal sauce which accompanies fried vegetables, fried fish, and, in particular, salted cod, to make a meal which is enjoyed by Greek islanders. In antiquity, garlic sauces travelled around the Mediterranean with the seafaring Greeks and appear as far from Greece as Provence and Andalucia under different guises and names. However, they all stem from Skorothalmi, a favorite of ancient Athenians.

---

4 medium slices white bread, soaked in water for 10 minutes
3 cloves garlic, peeled and chopped
1 tsp white wine vinegar
5 tbsp olive oil
1 tbsp ground walnuts or ground almonds (optional)
salt

Soak the bread in water for 10 minutes then squeeze to get rid of some of the water. Place it in a blender with the garlic, vinegar, and salt and blend till smooth. Add the olive oil slowly while blades are in motion. Add nuts if they are used and blend briefly. The sauce should have the consistency of mayonnaise. It is served on top of the fried vegetables or fish. It can also be served separately as a dip in a bowl accompanied by raw vegetables.

Horiatiki Salata

Mixed Salad

Lunch outdoors, particularly in the shade of a vine or an olive tree, is a setting for a substantial summer salad that could make a meal by itself. Ripe, sugary summer tomatoes are essential to its taste.

---

1 lb tomatoes, rinsed and dried
2 shallots, peeled and finely sliced
1 green pepper, rinsed, trimmed, and sliced in thin ribbons
4 in cucumber, peeled and thinly sliced
handful black or green olives
4 oz feta cheese, cubed
large pinch of dried oregano
6 tbsp fruity olive oil
salt

Slice the tomatoes in half and trim them. Quarter them and mix with all the ingredients in a large bowl. Toss gently to coat everything in the olive oil and serve with fresh, crusty bread for dipping into the juices.

Kolokythakia Salata

Courgette Salad

A deliciously refreshing dish, especially when courgettes are young and fresh, this can accompany grills, roasts, or fried fish or it can be served as a salad.

---

1 lb young firm courgettes
salt
5-6 tbsp fruity olive oil
2 tbsp lemon juice
parsley or fresh dill, finely chopped
salt and freshly ground pepper

Top and tail courgettes. Rinse and scrape them lightly under running water. Boil them whole in lightly salted boiling water for 10-12 minutes. Strain and place on a platter. Beat oil with remaining ingredients and pour over the courgettes. They are best served hot, but they can also be served at room temperature.

Fasolia Salata

Haricot Bean Salad

There is an inherent love for beans in Greece and people will go a long way to buy a tasty batch. They make a substantial dish served as a main meal augmented with fried fish or squid, particularly during Lent.

---

1 cup cannellini or haricot beans, picked clean
3-4 small shallots, peeled and sliced
3 tbsp chopped parsley
6-7 tbsp olive oil
juice of a lemon
salt and black pepper
black olives
2 hard-boiled eggs, peeled and quartered lengthwise

Soak beans overnight, rinse and cover with plenty of water. Bring to a boil, skim, cover, and cook until soft, about 40-50 minutes. If they are not to be eaten immediately, undercook them and let them stay in their liquid. Drain them just before they are to be served and place in a bowl with the shallots, parsley, and 2-3 tablespoons of their cooking liquid. Beat dressing ingredients lightly, add to the beans, and toss gently. Empty on a flat platter and garnish with the olives and the egg quarters.

Fasolatha

Canellini Bean Soup

Fasolatha is the national Greek dish. It has nourished generations. In the Greek islands it is as ubiquitous as the olive. Easy to cook, vegetarian, and nourishing, it is a very popular dish. Olive oil is one of the vital ingredients of this delicious dish so do not economize with it. Serve with olives or savory pickled fish such as anchovies.

---

1 cup cannellini or haricot beans, picked clean and soaked overnight
1 medium onion, finely sliced
2 small carrots, trimmed and thinly sliced
1 stick celery, trimmed, rinsed and finely sliced
14 oz can of tomatoes, chopped
1 tbsp tomato purée
1 tsp each oregano and thyme
½ cup olive oil
3 cups water
2 tbsp chopped parsley
salt and freshly ground pepper
(serves 6)

Rinse and strain beans. Place in a large saucepan, cover with water, and boil for 2-3 minutes. Drain, discarding the water. This step safeguards against flatulence and makes beans digestible. Cover the beans with 3 cups fresh water, bring to a boil and add remaining ingredients, except for the parsley. Cover and cook for about 50-60 minutes until the beans are soft. If using a pressure cooker, cook for 3-4 minutes only under 15 lb pressure. Mix the parsley in when the beans are cooked.

Dolmathakia

Stuffed Vine Leaves

Every garden in Greece has a *klimataria* – vine – providing shade from the dazzling summer sun and offering its young leaves in the early spring for culinary pleasure. Dolmathes are vine leaves stuffed with rice, onions, and fragrant olive oil – often the produce of the family – and, most importantly, the fresh herbs of the Greek hillsides, such as wild fennel, dill, and mint. The time-consuming task of rolling each leaf into a neat little parcel is supported and enhanced by little cups of steaming Greek coffee and the chatter of the women livens up as the morning proceeds. This is one of the most pleasurable of Greek dishes and one that epitomizes Greek life. This quantity will feed four as a main dish or six as a first course.

8 oz fresh or preserved vine leaves, (around 50)	3 tbsp dill, finely chopped
¾ cup long-grain rice, soaked, rinsed and drained	2 tbsp fresh mint, finely chopped
2 oz pine nuts, toasted lightly in a dry frying pan	3 tbsp parsley, chopped finely
	½ cup olive oil
10 oz onions and 3-4 spring onions	1 lemon
	1 cup hot water
	salt and black pepper

Rinse fresh vine leaves and plunge a few at a time briefly in a saucepan of boiling water to make them pliable. Remove with a slotted spoon and drain. If using salty preserved leaves rinse them 2-3 times and then soak them in a bowl of hot water for 3-4 minutes. Then rinse again and drain. Chop the onions finely or put them through a food processor briefly. Do not liquidize them. Mix all the ingredients, except water, in a large bowl, with half the olive

oil and half the lemon juice. Line the bottom of a wide saucepan with some of the vine leaves. Spread out a vine leaf, uneven side up. Place a tablespoon of stuffing near its serrated end, fold the stem ends over it, then both sides inwards and roll, forming a cigar-shaped parcel. Repeat with the rest of the vine leaves. Place them in the saucepan in tight circles, trapping loose ends underneath. Pour the rest of the olive oil, the lemon juice, and seasoning on top. Put a small inverted plate on the surface, in order to keep the rolls in place. Add the water, cover, and cook gently for 50 minutes. The Dolmathes can be served hot or cold, garnished with quartered lemons. Plain yogurt can be served as a sauce.

Briami

Baked Courgettes with Potatoes and Tomatoes

When served with Tzatziki, a bowl of olives, and some sharp feta cheese this is a refreshing and easy dish. It constitutes a meal in itself.

1 lb courgettes, trimmed and rinsed	1 green pepper, rinsed, trimmed, and sliced thinly
14 oz potatoes, peeled and cubed	large handful parsley, rinsed and chopped
14 oz can of tomatoes, finely chopped	½ cup olive oil
3 cloves garlic, peeled and sliced	½ cup hot water
1 small onion, peeled and finely sliced	large pinch oregano
	salt and freshly ground pepper

Slice courgettes into thin rounds. Mix with all the ingredients in a large roasting dish and bake in a pre-heated oven at 385°F for 1½ hours. Stir the vegetables a couple of times during cooking.

Yiemista

Stuffed Vegetables

Stuffed vegetables are the epitome of Greek summer life. Large shallow round containers with colorful contents are carried to and from the local bakers. When lunchtime comes, the bakers' kitchens are redolent with tantalizing aromas and full of color.

4 large tomatoes	1 tbsp tomato purée, diluted
4 green bell peppers	in ¾ cup hot water
½ tsp sugar	½ tsp dried oregano, or
5 tbsps olive oil	Greek rigani

Stuffing

2 medium onions, finely sliced	2 oz pine nuts, toasted lightly
½ cup olive oil	in a dry frying pan
1 small aubergine, peeled,	3 tbsp fresh mint or dill, finely
trimmed and cubed	chopped
1 cup long-grain rice,	4 tbsp parsley, finely chopped
rinsed and drained	salt and freshly ground pepper

Cut a round from the top of each tomato and pepper and reserve for sealing. Seed peppers, scoop most of the tomato flesh out with a teaspoon, chop, and reserve it for the stuffing. Invert tomatoes on a plate to drain but reserve their juices for the stuffing. Sprinkle a little sugar into each tomato before stuffing it. Brown the onions lightly in hot oil in a frying pan. Add the aubergine and sauté together briefly. Mix with remaining stuffing ingredients and the reserved tomato flesh. Fill each vegetable lightly and arrange upright in a baking dish. Seal with the reserved tops, pour over the tomato paste and 5 tablespoons of olive oil, sprinkle with the oregano and seasoning, and cook in a pre-heated oven, at 375°F for 1½ hours, basting occasionally. This dish can be served hot or at room temperature.

Fasolakia Freska

Green Bean Casserole

This is a simple but enticing casserole that can be served on its own for a light lunch or with fried Keftethes. Bobby beans, dwarf beans, and French beans are all excellent for this dish and they do not need stringing. Some feta cheese and black olives will add a very Greek touch.

---

1 lb fresh beans, topped and tailed
1 large onion, finely sliced
2 medium potatoes, peeled and cubed
2 cloves garlic, finely sliced
1 cup olive oil
14 oz can of tomatoes, chopped
salt and freshly ground pepper

Slice beans in halves, rinse, and drain. Sauté onion and garlic in hot oil until pale golden. Add beans and potatoes and sauté together until well-coated in the oil. Add the tomatoes and some seasoning. Cover and cook for about 30-40 minutes or until beans are tender, stirring occasionally. If needed, add a little hot water. This can be served hot or at room temperature.

Imam Bayildi

The Imam Fainted

The excessive amounts of olive oil in this dish may have been the cause of the Imam's fainting. But it is not clear whether he fainted out of meanness or delight. A delicious dish!

---

4 aubergines (about 2 lb)
½ cup or more vegetable oil for frying
10 oz onions, finely sliced
3 cloves garlic, finely sliced
4 tbsp olive oil
1 lb tomatoes, peeled and chopped (or a 14 oz can)
1 tsp dried oregano
4 tbsp parsley, finely chopped
1 tsp tomato purée diluted in a teacup of hot water
salt and black pepper

Rinse and dry the aubergines. Slit them on one side lengthwise, like a pouch. Fry them whole, turning them over and pressing them open on their split sides like a kite, until the inside is light golden. Drain on absorbent paper. Arrange the aubergines side by side in a medium-sized oven dish and season. Sauté onions in the olive oil until transparent, add garlic, and stir briefly until aromatic. Add tomatoes, herbs, and seasoning and cook for 15 minutes. If using canned tomatoes, chop them but keep most of the juice. Fill the pouch of the aubergines with this sauce. Add the reserved tomato juice to the pan or, if fresh tomatoes have been used, the diluted tomato purée. Bake at 350°F for 50-60 minutes, basting occasionally.

Kalamarakia Krasata

Squid in Wine Sauce

An easy way to cook squid, but this dish is unfailingly impressive. Medium-sized or large squid are best. It can be served as a main meal with rice or pasta, or on its own as a first course with fresh bread to mop up the enticingly sweet sauce.

---

2 lbs squid
5 tbsp olive or vegetable oil
1 lb onions, sliced
¼ cup white wine
½ cup water
2 small tomatoes, skinned and chopped
1 teaspoon oregano
salt and freshly ground pepper

Clean squid by pulling the heads away from the body. Slit the body lengthwise, empty and discard all the innards. Rinse away any trace of sand and drain. Cut off the upper part of the head just underneath the eyes, being careful not to splash yourself with the ink, and discard. Keep the ribbon-like strip with the tentacles attached to it, rinse well, and drain. Slice the bodies into 1 in strips. Heat the oil and sauté the onions until transparent, raise heat, add squid and fry fiercely, stirring, until all the liquid has evaporated and the squid starts to stick. Pour the wine in slowly and add the water with herbs and seasoning. Cover and simmer for 30 minutes, stirring occasionally to prevent sticking. Add the tomatoes and cook for a further 5-6 minutes until the squid is coated in a smooth velvety sauce.

Psari Spetsiota

Baked Fish in the Style of Spetsai Island

The entrancing little island of Spetsai in Saronikos Bay near Athens, with its traditional neo-classical houses overhung with scarlet bougainvillea flowers, has contributed this simple but mouth-watering dish to Greek culinary tradition. Tuna or swordfish steaks are often cooked in the same manner and while this recipe uses cod, hake or turbot could be used.

---

4 cod steaks (about 2 lb)
6 tbsp olive oil
3 cloves garlic, finely sliced
4 tbsp finely chopped parsley
I lb tomatoes, peeled, seeded, and finely chopped
salt and black pepper
2 tbsp freshly-made toasted breadcrumbs

Pat fish dry and arrange in one layer in a small oiled baking dish. Beat together all the ingredients except the breadcrumbs and spread over each slice. Make breadcrumbs by toasting 2-3 slices of bread, removing crusts, and processing briefly in a food processor. Sprinkle over the fish and cook in a pre-heated oven at 375°F for 30 minutes, basting occasionally until golden and crisp on top. Serve with a green salad or a salad of boiled courgettes.

Psarosoupa Avgolemono

Fish Soup with Egg and Lemon Sauce

This is one of the best dishes to have on a Greek island. You choose your fish at a *taverna* and the soup is cooked specially for you there and then. Some of the best fish for soup in Greece are the red *skorpina* (scorpion fish), the dark brown, big-headed *rofos* (grouper), the green *hristopsara* (John Dory), *sfyritha* (Mérou Blanc), silvery *lavraki* (sea bass), and *kefalos* (grey mullet), but of course we can improvise and substitute. A good combination of fish to use is conger eel and monkfish or whole red gurnard, monkfish with halibut or whiting, or a whole sea bass. Allow at least 8 oz of fish per person or more if whole fish is used. This soup may be served with or without the egg and lemon sauce.

3-4 lbs fish steaks or whole fish	4 small carrots, scraped
4 cups fish stock or water	2 stick celery, washed, and cut into 2 in pieces
5 tbsp olive oil	4-5 small onions, peeled
6 small potatoes, peeled	3 stalks parsley, washed
	salt

Avgolemono Sauce

2 eggs	1½ lemons

Bring water, olive oil, and salt to a boil in a large saucepan. Add the vegetables and cook for 15 minutes. Add the fish, bring to a boil, skim, cover, and cook gently for 15-20 minutes. Remove from heat and let it rest for five minutes. Take fish out carefully, lay on a platter surrounded by the vegetables, and keep warm. Beat the eggs with the lemon juice. Gradually add ½ cup of the hot (but not boiling) broth. Add this slowly to the soup while turning the pan. Gently reheat, stirring to avoid curdling. Serve the soup with the fish and vegetables.

Arnaki Frikassee

Lamb and Romaine Lettuce Casserole

Predominantly an Easter and Spring dish that has the taste of milk-fed lamb and young greenery, this dish includes spring onions, tender lettuces, and feathery aromatic bunches of dill. It uses many of the same ingredients as *magiritsa* (the soup that breaks the Lent fast after the midnight resurrection liturgy on Saturday). Ideally it should be made with a leg of lamb, but a lean boned shoulder can be used. Serve with fresh bread to mop up the wonderful sauce.

1 medium onion, finely sliced	4 tbsp vegetable oil
5-6 spring onions, trimmed, rinsed and chopped	3 cups hot water
3 lb leg or shoulder of lamb, boned, trimmed of fat, and cut into serving portions	2 heads romaine lettuce, washed, strained, and shredded
	4 tbsp fresh dill, chopped
	salt

Avgolemono Sauce

3 eggs   2 large lemons

(serves 6)

Rinse and dry meat. Sauté the onions in the hot oil until transparent, raise heat, add the meat, and stir until all liquid evaporates and starts to stick (about 10-15 minutes). Add water and salt, cover, and cook gently for 45-50 minutes until meat is tender. Add lettuce and dill, reserving a little of the dill for garnishing, and mix. Cover and cook gently for 15 minutes. Take from heat and rest for five minutes before adding the sauce. Beat the eggs lightly, add lemon juice, and beat together briefly. Gradually add 5-6 tablespoons of the hot (but not boiling) sauce. Pour this slowly over the meat, turning the pan to make sure meat is covered. Heat very gently for 3-4 minutes without boiling to warm the sauce through.

Moshari Stifatho

Beef Casserole with Baby Onions

This is a hearty and extremely tasty winter dish. It can also be made with all kinds of game such as hare or rabbit or even with octopus. Serve it with fresh bread and a winter salad of sliced white cabbage or a mixed green salad.

---

3 lb brisket or braising steak, cut in large cubes
6 tbsp olive oil
4 tbsp red wine vinegar
small glass red wine
small cinnamon stick
3-4 grains allspice
small sprig rosemary
3 cups water
salt and freshly ground pepper
1 teaspoon brown sugar
1 ½ lb shallots or small onions, peeled whole
(serves 4-6)

Brown the meat in the hot oil. Pour the wine and the vinegar over it slowly until the steam subsides. Mix in remaining ingredients except for sugar and onions. Cover and cook slowly for about one hour or until the meat is almost tender. Spread the shallots over the meat evenly. Add a little water if needed. Sprinkle the sugar over the onions, cover, and simmer for a further half hour until the onions are soft. Do not stir once the onions have been added but turn and shake the saucepan to coat them in the sauce.

Kotopitta

Chicken Pie

A delicious dish with a subtle and light taste, this is an excellent choice for a buffet or a summer lunch outdoors. The chicken can be prepared a day in advance to simplify the task.

1 boiling chicken about 3 lb, quartered	3 eggs
10 oz onions, peeled and sliced	white pepper
salt	2-3 tbsp dill or parsley, finely chopped
2 tbsp grated Parmesan or Gruyere cheese	1 lb pkt fyllo pastry
	1 stick butter, melted
(serves 6-8)	

Rinse the chicken in cold water. Place in large saucepan, cover with water, and a little salt, bring to a boil and skim until clear. Add onions, cover, and cook until chicken is tender. Lift the chicken out and boil the liquid rapidly to reduce it to about 1 cup. Skin and bone the chicken, shred the meat, and put back into the liquid. This can wait now for up to 24 hours if needed. Beat the eggs lightly, add the cheese, dill, and seasoning and mix in with the chicken. Brush the inside of a large oblong oven dish with melted butter. Defrost pastry, if needed, and keep covered with a damp cloth as it dries out quickly. Brush a sheet of pastry with melted butter and line the bottom of the baking dish. Repeat until half the pastry is used. Spread the chicken filling evenly over the pastry and cover with remaining leaves, brushing each sheet with butter. Fold in the edges of pastry neatly or cut with scissors if too long. Cut the top layers of pastry only into square serving portions. Sprinkle a little cold water over the top and bake in a pre-heated oven at 375°F for

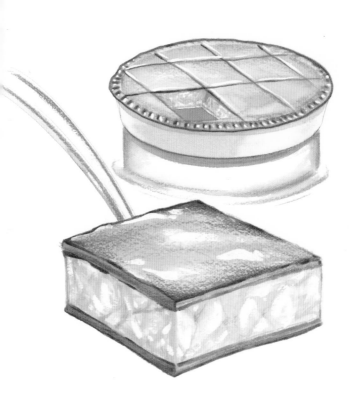

40-45 minutes until golden. Let it stand for 10 minutes before cutting and serving. Serve with a crisp green salad.

Moussaka

Moussaka is identified with Greek summer life. It is time-consuming to prepare but worth the effort, absolutely delicious when freshly made, and economical as it can easily feed a whole family. As it is quite rich serve it with sharp feta cheese and a salad or a Horiatiki Salata (see page 16).

---

2 lb aubergines, trimmed and sliced in 1/4 in thick slices	14 oz can of tomatoes, finely chopped
1 cup sunflower oil	1/4 tsp ground cinnamon
1 large onion, finely chopped	1 tsp dried oregano
1 lb minced beef or lamb or a mixture of both	salt and freshly ground pepper

Bechamel Sauce

2 cups warm milk	salt
3/4 stick butter	1 egg yolk, lightly beaten
1/4 cup plain flour	

Topping

2 tbsp grated Parmesan cheese

(serves 6)

Immerse aubergine slices in lightly salted water for 20-30 minutes to extract their bitterness. Rinse, squeezing them gently, and pat them dry. Reserve a little of the oil. Heat the rest and fry the aubergines until light golden on both sides. Drain them on absorbent paper. In the meantime, sauté the onion in the reserved oil until transparent. Add meat and sauté until it starts to brown. Add remaining ingredients, mix, cover, and cook for 20-30 minutes, until quite dry. To make the sauce, melt the butter in a heavy saucepan, add flour gradually, and stir until well incorporated. Remove from heat and add the warm milk while stirring. Return to heat, add salt, and keep stirring until thickened, about 10 minutes. Take from heat and add the egg yolk, stirring continuously. Line a medium-sized baking dish (approx. 10 x 10 in) with the aubergine slices. Season them, spread the meat evenly over them, and cover with the béchamel. Sprinkle cheese on top and cook in a pre-heated oven at 350°F for about 50 minutes until crisp and golden. Let it rest for 10 minutes, then cut in squares and serve.

Kotopoulo Fournou

Roast Chicken with Potatoes

This is a delicious and easy way to cook several things together as the potatoes cook in the tasty juices of the chicken and the lemon. The chicken and potatoes should be crisp and golden by the end of the cooking.

3 lb free-range or corn-fed chicken	2½ sticks butter
2 lb potatoes, peeled and sliced	salt and freshly ground pepper
	1 tbsp oregano
juice of a large lemon	½ cup hot water
4 tbsp olive oil	

Place the chicken in a large roasting pan, breast down and surround it with the potatoes. Pour on the olive oil and lemon juice, dot with butter, season, and sprinkle with herbs. Pour the water in a corner of the pan and roast in a pre-heated oven, at 425°F for 30 minutes. Take out, turn the chicken over, and baste. Sprinkle on remaining

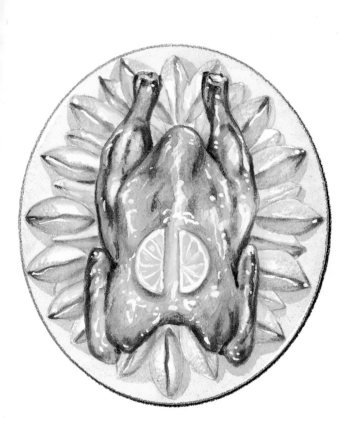

herbs and cook for another hour, checking in case it needs a little more water. The chicken should be quite golden by the end. Serve with a crisp green salad.

Giouvetsi

Baked Lamb or Goat with Pasta

This is *the* celebratory Greek dish reserved for large family gatherings, weddings, namedays, and particularly the 15th of August when all the women named Maria and the men named Panagiotis celebrate. Usually, the treasured family baby goat is slaughtered for the occasion. Once the pasta is cooked, the meal should be consumed immediately.

---

3 lb boned leg or shoulder of lamb or goat, sliced into serving portions
½ cup hot water
4 cloves garlic, peeled and halved
14 oz can of tomatoes or 1 lb fresh tomatoes, finely chopped
6 tbsp olive oil
1 tbsp dried oregano or Greek rigani
salt and freshly ground pepper
12 oz orzo – small tear-shaped pasta – the Greek kritharaki, or spaghetti
(serves 6)

Wipe meat and place it in a roasting dish with the garlic and water. Pour over olive oil, tomatoes, seasonings, and oregano. Cook in a pre-heated oven at 425°F for 50 minutes, basting from time to time, and turning pieces over. Add 1 cup boiling water, seasoning, and the pasta. Turn the oven down to 400°F and bake for another

40 minutes until the pasta is cooked to taste, stirring occasionally.
If needed, add a little more hot water.

Kotopoulo me Bamies

Chicken and Okra Casserole

My mother always sends a huge container of this casserole to the
local baker the day after we arrive in Athens for our summer
holiday. It is an easy dish to make and adds glamour to the chicken
as well as to the occasion.

---

5 tbsp olive oil
3 1/2 lb free-range chicken, jointed
1 large onion, finely sliced
14 oz can of tomatoes, finely chopped
1 tsp tomato paste
1/2 cup water
1 tbsp oregano
1 1/2 lb okra
salt and freshly ground pepper

Rinse, dry, and lightly brown chicken pieces in the hot oil in a large
saucepan. Remove chicken, add onion, and when golden, put
chicken pieces back with the tomatoes, tomato paste, herbs,
seasoning and water. Cover and cook for 20-30 minutes. Prepare
okra by peeling the heads thinly without bruising. Rinse gently in a
bowl of cold water and drain. Spread the okra evenly over the
chicken and shake the casserole a little. Add more seasoning, cover
and cook gently for 30 more minutes. Once the okra has been
added do not stir; shake and turn the saucepan instead.

Baklavas

This is a spectacular dessert with simple ingredients. Honeyed walnuts, however, make it absolutely delicious. Baklavas is quite easy to make and suitable for a large gathering but you do need to master handling the ready-made, paper-thin Greek fyllo pastry.

Filling

1 lb walnuts, coarsely chopped	3 tbsp sugar
	½ tsp cinnamon

Pastry

1 lb pkt fyllo pastry	1½ sticks unsalted butter, melted

Syrup

1½ cups sugar	2-3 cloves
2½ cups water	1 tbsp lemon juice
1 large cinnamon stick	2 tbsp clear honey

(serves 10-12)

Defrost pastry, if needed, and keep it covered with a damp cloth as it dries out quickly. Mix all the filling ingredients in a bowl. Butter the base of a large oblong roasting pan (approximately 15 in x 10 in) and cover it neatly with 5-6 sheets of pastry, brushing each layer with melted butter before lifting it from the stack. Fold in excess length of each sheet at alternative ends. Spread half of the filling evenly over the pastry and cover with 3 more layers of buttered pastry. Spread over remaining filling and then fold over all the edges enclosing the filling neatly. Butter each sheet of remaining pastry and cover the top neatly. Cut away excess pastry all round the edges. Cut the top layers of the baklava into small oblong or diamond portions in order to facilitate serving once it has been cooked. Sprinkle on a little cold water with the tips of your fingers to prevent the edges curling up and cook in a pre-heated oven at

350°F for 25-30 minutes. Turn heat up to 375°F and cook for another 10-15 minutes until light golden. Let it cool before adding the syrup. Mix the syrup ingredients except for honey and boil for 8-10 minutes. Add honey and simmer for another 5 minutes until slightly thickened. Discard cinnamon and cloves and pour the syrup slowly over the baklava. Let it stand for 10 minutes until all the syrup has been absorbed and it looks glossy on top. If covered to prevent drying, it will keep well at room temperature for 2-3 days.

Loukoumathes

Honeyed Crisp Doughnuts

Perfectly round, crisp Loukoumathes were a treat after a rare visit to the central food market in Athens with my mother or a Sunday outing. Although made with simple ingredients they have an enticing combination of tastes and textures.

1 tsp easy-blend dried yeast	vegetable oil for deep frying
1 cup warm water	6 tbsp thyme-scented Greek
1 cup plain flour	honey
large pinch salt	½ tsp ground cinnamon
(serves 6-7)	

Sift flour with salt in a bowl and mix it with the dried yeast. Add the warm water slowly and beat until the mixture is smooth and frothy. Cover with a tea towel and let it rest in a warm place for an hour until it doubles. Heat the oil to just under smoking point in a deep-fryer and drop teaspoons of the mixture in it, about six at a time. Dip the teaspoon in cold water between each amount to prevent dough sticking. The doughnuts puff up and rise to the surface within seconds. Turn them and when they acquire a pale

golden color, lift them out with a slotted spoon and drain on absorbent paper. This quantity will produce about thirty Loukoumathes. Dribble a tablespoon of honey over them, sprinkle with cinnamon and serve immediately, 4-5 per person.

Kourabiethes

Shortbread Christmas Cakes

Snowy, half-moon shaped Kourabiethes make their appearance in *zaharoplastia* (cake shops) around November. They can be seen in huge sugar-dusted mounds everywhere just before Christmas.

1 lb unsalted butter	8 oz shelled almonds,
1 cup superfine sugar	slightly toasted and coarsely
3 egg yolks	chopped
4 tbsp brandy	2 lb self-rising flour
4-5 drops pure vanilla essence	3 tbsp rosewater
	1½ cups icing sugar

Cream butter, add sugar and beat together. Beat in the egg yolks and then brandy and vanilla. Add the sifted flour and the almonds and mix well. Knead quickly. It should be quite a stiff dough. If it feels sticky, add a little more flour. Roll out the pastry on a cool surface to ¼ in thickness and using pastry cutters, cut half-moon, round, or star shapes (about 24-26 pieces). Place cakes on a greased baking sheet and cook in a pre-heated oven at 375°F for 20 minutes until a creamy color. Do not let them brown. Cool and sprinkle with a little rosewater. Put on platter that has been dusted with some icing sugar and sprinkle the remaining icing sugar over them.

Index